OWLS IN THE DARK

Doreen Gonzales

PowerKiDS
press.

New York

Published in 2010 by The Rosen Publishing Group, Inc.
29 East 21st Street, New York, NY 10010

First Edition

Editor: Amelie von Zumbusch
Book Design: Julio Gil
Photo Researcher: Jessica Gerweck

Photo Credits: Cover Joe McDonald/Getty Images; p. 5 Kim Wolhuter/Getty Images; p. 6 © Ron Austing; Frank Lane Picture Agency/Corbis; p. 9 © Myron Jay Dorf/Corbis; pp. 10, 13 Joe McDonald/Corbis; p. 14 Masami Goto/Sebun Photo/Getty Images; p. 17 © Herbert Spichtinger/zefa/Corbis; p. 18 Shutterstock.com; p. 21 Art Wolfe/Getty Images.

Library of Congress Cataloging-in-Publication Data

Gonzales, Doreen.
  Owls in the dark / Doreen Gonzales. — 1st ed.
    p. cm. — (Creatures of the night)
  Includes index.
  ISBN 978-1-4042-8097-7 (library binding) — ISBN 978-1-4358-3251-0 (pbk.) —
ISBN 978-1-4358-3252-7 (6-pack)
  1. Owls—Juvenile literature. I. Title.
  QL696.S8G66 2010
  598.9'7—dc22

                                    2008054865

Manufactured in the United States of America

Contents

CAN YOU HEAR THAT?

Take a walk in your front yard and step on a stick. Can you hear it snap? An owl sitting in a tree across the street could! Owls have excellent hearing. Owls are raptors, or birds that hunt other animals.

Most owls are **nocturnal**. These owls hunt at night. Other owls are **crepuscular**. This means they hunt at **dawn** and **dusk**. A few kinds of owls hunt during the day.

Owls are covered in long, soft feathers. Some owls have **tufts** of feathers on their heads. These tufts are often called ears or horns.

This owl's tufts look like ears, but the bird's ears are really hidden under its feathers. The owl's excellent hearing lets it hunt at night, when it is too dark to see much.

OWLS ARE EVERYWHERE!

Owls can be found almost everywhere in the world. There are more than 200 kinds of owls. Elf owls are the smallest kind. They are only 6 inches (15 cm) long. Two of the largest owls are the great gray owl and the great horned owl. These owls' wings can measure 5 feet (1.5 m) from tip to tip.

Some kinds of owls can live only in one kind of place. For example, many kinds of spotted owls live only in forests of very old trees. Burrowing owls live under the ground in homes left by squirrels or foxes. Other types of owls live in many kinds of places. For example, barn owls live in deserts, forests, wetlands, and grasslands.

Elf owls live in Mexico and the American Southwest. These tiny owls often make their homes in cacti, like this one.

Built for the Night

Owls are built for night hunting. Their big eyes take in all the light around them. This lets owls see in dim light, such as moonlight. Owls cannot turn their eyes in their heads, as people do. However, owls can turn their heads nearly all the way around to get a view of their **surroundings**. Owls often see **prey** that cannot see them.

Owls also use their hearing to find prey. The feathers that circle an owl's face direct sounds to the bird's ears. Many owls can hear prey they cannot see, such as animals under snow.

Owls can see well both during the day and at night. However, owls cannot see colors as well as people do.

WITHOUT A SOUND

An owl's wings help make it a good hunter, too. Owls have large wings, which the birds do not need to flap much to stay in the air. The feathers on these wings have soft edges, which quiet the sound of air moving through them. Their big, soft wings let owls fly without making any noise. This means owls can get near their prey without ever being heard.

Owls catch many kinds of prey. Many owls catch mice. Some owls eat fish and frogs. The smallest owls eat bugs and worms. Large owls often eat rabbits, squirrels, and birds.

Eastern screech owls, such as this bird, beat their wings about five times per second. This is fairly fast for an owl.

THE HUNT

Different owls hunt in different ways. Some owls fly quietly over the ground looking for food. Others sit on low branches to watch and listen for prey.

Once prey is discovered, an owl dives down and catches the animal in its **talons**. Then, the owl lifts the prey to its **beak**, which curls down to help the bird hold its food. These raptors often swallow their prey whole. Several hours after they have finished eating, owls spit up balls of bones, fur, and other things that their bodies cannot break down. These balls are shaped like little hot dogs and are called pellets.

This great gray owl is about to catch a mouse. Though great gray owls are large, they eat mostly small mammals, such as mice and voles.

An Owl's Life

Most owls do not build nests. Instead, the birds often live in dead trees, caves, and barns. Some owls live in the old nests of large birds, such as crows. Many owls have brown spots on their feathers. This makes the birds in their shadowy nests hard to see and keeps them safe during the day.

Owls make many sounds. They hoot, scream, and click their beaks. Each kind of owl has its own song. Owls use sounds and songs to talk with other owls. This is useful to nocturnal owls, since the birds cannot always see each other as they hunt.

Several kinds of owls have striped fronts. Their stripes make the birds hard to see against certain kinds of trees.

CHICKS

As all birds do, baby owls **hatch** from eggs. Owl eggs are round and white. Most mother owls lay 3 or 4 eggs at a time, though some owls lay up to 12 eggs. Mothers stay at their nests keeping the eggs warm. Father owls bring the mothers food.

Baby owls are called chicks. Newly hatched owl chicks cannot see and are covered with thick white **down**. As the babies grow, they get new feathers. After 4 to 10 weeks, the chicks start flying. Owls take good care of their chicks. They chase animals and people away from their young, striking those who come near with their talons.

Before they learn to fly, owl chicks must learn to climb out of their nests and walk along nearby cliffs or tree branches.

The Great Horned Owl

One of the best-known owls is the great horned owl. It lives in deserts, forests, and cliffs all over North America and South America. The great horned owl gets its name from the tufts of feathers on its head. These large owls may be 2 feet (61 cm) long and can weigh 5 pounds (2 kg). Great horned owls are brown with a bib of white feathers. They have large yellow eyes.

Great horned owls hunt mostly at night. They eat rabbits, skunks, and many other animals. These big owls are known for their call. It sounds like "whoo whoo." Some great horned owl calls can be heard from several miles (km) away.

Great horned owls are one of the most common kinds of owls in North America and South America. They live in city parks, towns, farmlands, as well as wild places.

NORTHERN SAW-WHET OWLS

Many owls are known for the sounds they make. Northern saw-whet owls even get their name from their call. When male northern saw-whets are in danger, they make a call that sounds like "skiew." This reminds many people of a saw being whetted, or sharpened.

Northern saw-whet owls live in forests of the United States, southern Canada, and central Mexico. At night, the owls hunt for little animals, such as mice. These small owls are generally between 7 and 8.5 inches (18–22 cm) long. Male northern saw-whets are smaller than females, as is often the case among owls.

As several kinds of owls do, northern saw-whet owls have feathers covering their feet. These keep them warm in the winter.

OWLS FOR TOMORROW

People have been interested in owls for thousands of years. In the past, people thought these birds had magical powers. Some believed owls brought bad luck. Other people thought owls were wise.

Today, we know that owls are not magic. However, these wonderful birds are helpful to us. For example, owls eat animals, such as mice and rats, that eat crops and bother people.

We can help owls by making sure they have lots of open places in which to live. We can also build boxes in trees for owls to use as nests. In this way, we can make sure owls will always be around.

GLOSSARY

BEAK (BEEK) The hard mouth of a bird or a turtle.

CREPUSCULAR (krih-PUS-kyuh-lur) Active just before sunrise and just after sunset.

DAWN (DAHN) The period of dim light before the Sun rises.

DOWN (DOWN) A covering of soft, fluffy feathers.

DUSK (DUSK) The period of dim light after the Sun sets.

HATCH (HACH) To come out of an egg.

NOCTURNAL (nok-TUR-nul) Active during the night.

PREY (PRAY) Animals that are hunted by another animal for food.

SURROUNDINGS (suh-ROWN-dingz) The land or space on all sides of something.

TALONS (TA-lunz) The strong, sharp-clawed feet of a bird that eats animals.

TUFTS (TUFTS) Batches of hair, grass, or other things that are fixed to something at one end.

INDEX

A
animal(s), 4, 8, 12, 16, 19, 20, 22

B
beak(s), 12, 15
bird(s), 4, 11–12, 15–16, 22

D
dusk, 4

E
ears, 4, 8

F
feathers, 4, 8, 11, 15–16, 19

H
head(s), 4, 8, 19
hearing, 4, 8
horns, 4

P
prey, 8, 11–12

R
raptors, 4, 12

S
surroundings, 8

T
talons, 12, 16
tree(s), 4, 7, 15, 22
tufts, 4, 19

W
walk, 4
world, 7

Y
yard, 4

WEB SITES

Due to the changing nature of Internet links, PowerKids Press has developed an online list of Web sites related to the subject of this book. This site is updated regularly. Please use this link to access the list:
www.powerkidslinks.com/cnight/owl/